DIGGING DEEPER INTO THE REVELATION OF JESUS CHRIST

Study Guide

EXAM BOOKLET

Questions – Answers - References

MICHAEL COPPLE

E G Publishing Eternally Grateful

Copyright © 2025 by Michael Copple.

All rights reserved. No part of this book may be used or reproduced in any form whatsoever without written permission except in the case of brief quotations in critical articles or reviews.

This is a work of non-fiction.

Scripture quotations are taken from the New King James Version®. Copyright © 1982 by Thomas Nelson. Used by permission. All rights reserved.

Cover design by Ben Bredeweg / modifications for this booklet by Elfriede Copple

ISBN – Paperback: 978-1-7389735-9-0

Printed in the United States of America.

First Edition: January 2026

CONTENTS

INSTRUCTIONS FOR THE EXAMS	vi
CHAPTER EXAMS	1
CHAPTERS 1-3	3
CHAPTERS 4-7	7
CHAPTERS 8-10	11
CHAPTERS 11-13	15
CHAPTERS 14-16	19
CHAPTERS 17-19	23
CHAPTERS 20-22	27
FINAL EXAM	31
CHAPTER EXAM	
ANSWERS / REFERENCES	41
FINAL EXAM	
ANSWERS / REFERENCES	47
CONNECT WITH THE AUTHOR	53

INSTRUCTIONS FOR THE EXAMS

The 22 chapters in the Book of *The Revelation of Jesus Christ* have been divided into eight separate exams, seven for the Chapters and one Final Exam.

The seven Chapter Exams each consist of ten multiple choice questions and are distributed as follows:

Chapters 1-3;
Chapters 4-7;
Chapters 8-10;
Chapters 11-13;
Chapters 14-16;
Chapters 17-19; and
Chapters 20-22

The Final Exam covers all the chapters and has thirty multiple choice questions. In order to preserve each copy of the Exam Booklet, (and so that the exam can be passed on to others) rather than making a checkmark in the booklet, we recommend denoting the answers on a separate paper.

Unless your instructor or moderator gives different instructions, you may use your Bible for answering the questions. Upon finishing each exam, see the back of the exam booklet for the correct answers and biblical references.

REVELATION STUDY GUIDE

CHAPTER EXAMS

CHAPTERS 1-3

1. The person who reads and hears the words of prophecy in the Book of Revelation is:

    A. Blessed
    B. Gifted with teaching ability
    C. Gifted with discernment
    D. Invited to the Great White Throne Judgment Seat

2. *The Revelation of Jesus Christ*, is from whom and to whom?

    A. From John the Baptist to all churches
    B. From Paul to all the elders
    C. From John, Father God, seven Spirits; and Lord Jesus to the seven churches in Asia
    D. From John to the twenty-four elders

3. Every eye will see the Lord Jesus, even those who rejected Him during their life on earth.

    A. True
    B. False

4. John's vision of Jesus closely resembles which of the following prophet's vision of Him:

   A. Isaiah
   B. Hosea
   C. Zechariah
   D. Ezekiel

5. The Lord Jesus told John to tell the church of Pergamos how to return to Him by:

   A. Conducting a revival
   B. Repenting
   C. Worshiping with musical instruments
   D. Preaching how to get more material riches

6. The doctrines of Bālaam and the Nicōlāitans had what similarities?

   A. Idolatry, unity, and sexual immorality
   B. Idolatry, sexual immorality, and use of godliness for monetary gain
   C. Unity, monetary gain, and idolatry
   D. Appointing male elders and not allowing only one man to be over the laity

7. Jesus told the angel of the church in Smyrna, if faithful until death, He would give them:

   A. Wrath
   B. A painless death by beheading
   C. Sackcloth
   D. The crown of life

8. Jesus told the angel of the church in Sardis for them to:

   A. Hold Fast and repent
   B. Spread the Gospel Message
   C. Rest assured He would not blot our any of their names from the Book of Life
   D. Schedule a revival

9. Jesus told the angel of the church in Philadelphia:

   A. They had denied His name
   B. They had kept His word
   C. He would not keep them from the hour of trial
   D. They would be tested in the first half of the Tribulation Period

10. The word *churches* is repeated after Revelation chapter 4:1 and prior to 22:16.

    A. True
    B. False

CHAPTERS 4-7

1. The first words: After these things in Revelation 4:1 refer to:

   A. After the first three Covenant Ages of biblical history
   B. After the collapse of the Roman Empire
   C. After the Church Age
   D. After the Second Coming of Christ

2. The three passages having to do with the trumpet announcing the Rapture are found in:

   A. 2 Thessalonians 2:4-5, 1 Thessalonians 4:13-5:11, 1 Corinthians 15:51-52
   B. Revelation 4:1, 1 Thessalonians 4:13-5:11, Romans 11:25-26
   C. 1 Corinthians 15:51-52, 1 Thessalonians 4:13-5:11, Revelation 4:1
   D. Revelation 4:1, 1 Thessalonians 4:13-5:11, 2 Thessalonians 2:1-8

3. The first rewards given to the twenty-four elders for serving well were in the form of:

   A. Crowns of different sorts during the Millennial Reign
   B. Positions of authority during the Great Tribulation
   C. Time off after the revealing of the Antichrist
   D. Crowns of Gold soon after the Rapture of the Church

4. What are the raptured believers referred to when they praise the Lord for redeeming them?

   A. "Living creatures" in Revelation 5:11
   B. "Disciples" in John 18:2
   C. "Apostates" in 2 Peter 3 and Jude
   D. "Angels" in Revelation 5:8

5. The "living creatures" who recognize the Lord for redeeming them by His blood in Revelation 5:9-11 are

   A. The four living creatures in Revelation 5:8 only
   B. The Cherubim and Seraphim only
   C. The twenty-four elders of the Church only
   D. The ten thousand times ten thousand, and thousands of thousands made up of the many angels, the elders, and Christ's new creation which was recently raptured.

6. The four different colored horses in Revelation 6:2-8 represent:

   A. Four different prominent men entering the kingdom of God
   B. The Antichrist and his seven-year career during the Tribulation Period
   C. The Lord Jesus, Satan, the Antichrist, and the False Prophet
   D. Four kings of the New World Governments

7. The white horse in Revelation 6:2 and the pale horse in verse 8 signify

   A. The Antichrist's promise for peace in the beginning and his death at the end
   B. The beginning and end of the war of Armageddon
   C. The Rapture, first 3½ years of troubles, Millennium, and new heaven and earth
   D. The different ages prior to Daniel's 70th week

8. The 144,000 Israelites are saved and sealed

   A. Prior to opening of the first six seals and after revealing of the Antichrist
   B. After the wedding of the Church to the Savior
   C. Prior to the seven-year Tribulation
   D. After the revealing of the Antichrist and after to the opening of the sixth seal

9. The 12,000 from each of twelve tribes of Israel were sealed

   A. In heaven
   B. In the New Jerusalem
   C. On earth
   D. None of the above

10. *After these things* in Revelation 7:9 a great multitude worshiping takes place at what time and place

    A. After the Tribulation Period at God's throne
    B. During the first half of the Tribulation Period in the wilderness
    C. Atop Mount Carmel at the end of the battle of Armageddon
    D. During the Great Tribulation in the city of Petra

CHAPTERS 8-10

1. Who opens the seventh seal in Chapter 8:1?

    A. The angel who will sound the first trumpet
    B. One of the elders
    C. The Lamb of God
    D. Either Elījah or Moses

2. Why was there silence in heaven for about half an hour when the seventh seal was opened?

    A. The intensity of God's wrath was about to be amplified
    B. Everyone was exhausted from so much prior praising and worshiping
    C. There was a mandatory waiting period before sounding the first trumpet
    D. The same angel who'd opened the seal now needed time to find the seventh trumpet

3. What caused one third of the earth's waters to be undrinkable when the third angel sounded his trumpet?

    A. Livestock infestation
    B. The Antichrist's intervention
    C. Wormwood
    D. The powers Satan gave to the False Prophet

4. What caused the sun and air to darken after the fifth angel sounded his trumpet?

   A. Smog from the great city of Babylon
   B. Smoke arose out of the bottomless pit
   C. Dark clouds
   D. The sun's intensity had greatly diminished

5. For five months the locusts having the power of scorpions will strike men and kill them

   A. True
   B. False

6. Trumpet six blasts the second woe which is

   A. Irritating noises like that of a band tuning its instruments
   B. All the men on earth experienced kidney failure
   C. A devastating tornado wiped out one third of the earth's cities
   D. Two hundred million horsemen kill a third of mankind

7. The remainder of mankind who were not killed after the sixth trumpet do the following:

   A. They do not repent of their murders; rather they continue to worship idols
   B. They do repent and become survivors of the Tribulation
   C. They flee and look for places to hide
   D. They join forces with the opposition that caused so many to die

8. The "little book" that the angel told John to "eat" represents

   A. Sweet overcoming for those who accept—and the bitter end for those who reject Him
   B. A mystery that is too sacred to be revealed
   C. The bitter beginning and sweet end of the Book of Job
   D. A poetic work of literature

9. When the seven thunders uttered their voices in Revelation 10:4 it signaled that there should be:

   A. A violent hurricane
   B. A torrential rain
   C. No more delay before God's unleashing of His wrath
   D. The sounding of the third and fourth trumpets

10. Even with all the warnings given so far, the angel on the sea and earth told John

    A. To take cover
    B. To prophesy again
    C. That it is too late to write any more
    D. None of the above

CHAPTERS 11-13

1. During the first half of the Tribulation, Jerusalem will be under the control of

    A. The Russian, Chinese, North Korean and Iranian military units
    B. The Jews
    C. The Gentiles
    D. All of the above

2. The two witnesses in Revelation could quite possibly be:

    A. Two of the 144,000 Israelites who were saved in Revelation 7
    B. The two prophets who appeared in the Transfiguration of Jesus' appearance
    C. Two of the Kings of the Northern Kingdom of Israel
    D. Adam and Eve, Job and his wife, or Āhab and Jezebel

3. In Revelation 11:3-12, eyewitnesses will see the two witnesses:

    A. Defeat the radical Islamic terrorists
    B. Perform healings among the many men with sores
    C. Repenting for falling away
    D. Ascending to heaven in a cloud

4. One dozen being twelve in English is comparable to one week being seven years in Hebrew.

   A. True
   B. False

5. In Revelation 12:2, the labor and pain in giving birth refers to:

   A. The tremendous pain that all pregnant women go through in childbearing
   B. The difficult situation for all people in the seven-year Tribulation
   C. The suffering Israel endured during the Church Age as they rejected Christ
   D. Mary's pains in giving birth both to Jesus and to His siblings who did not believe

6. After Israel was born again—saved and sealed in Revelation 7—what took place in chapter 12?

   A. A great, fiery red dragon drew a third of the stars of heaven to earth to devour them
   B. There was peace and serenity on the new earth
   C. The northern nations gave up, seeing that their chances were slim
   D. The United Nations declared a one world government

7. Michael and his angels fight a war with Satan in the following location:

   A. New York City
   B. Rome
   C. Babylon
   D. Heaven

8. The two beasts in Revelation 13 are

   A. Satan and the Antichrist
   B. The Antichrist and the False Prophet
   C. Satan and the False Prophet
   D. The wolf and the lamb

9. The Antichrist takes the place of the Messiah in the false trinity with the following deception:

   A. Long hair and a beard
   B. A deadly wound that was healed
   C. Success in bringing total peace
   D. Compassion for little children

10. For anyone who will not worship the image of the beast they would be

    A. Killed
    B. Given indoctrination training
    C. Given a six-month grace period
    D. Sent to prison

CHAPTERS 14-16

1. The hundred and forty-four thousand who were redeemed from *among* men were

    A. Raptured
    B. Relieved of responsibilities
    C. To preach the everlasting gospel to those who dwell on earth
    D. All sent to prison

2. The hundred and forty-four thousand who were redeemed were called first fruits because

    A. They were saved before anyone else
    B. They were the first mentioned to be saved during the Tribulation Period
    C. They were saved during the harvest season
    D. They were the first to recognize the Antichrist to be unfaithful

3. The Lord Jesus saw His Father's name written on the foreheads of the 144,000

    A. On Mount Zion
    B. In heaven
    C. In Babylon
    D. In Bethlehem

4. Whoever receives the mark of the name of the beast

   A. Will be given one more chance to repent
   B. Will enjoy their tranquility with the peace that's been promised
   C. Will be forgiven for making such a hasty decision
   D. Will be tormented forever and ever

5. The wrath of God will be completed with the following:

   A. The help of the Israeli Army and Air Force
   B. The United Nations valiant efforts to overthrow the Antichrist
   C. The Eastern and Western nations' leaders' new alliance
   D. Seven plagues contained in seven vials—or bowls

6. In Revelation 15:3, the song of Moses and the song of the Lamb depict

   A. God's deliverance from slavery in Egypt and deliverance from Satan
   B. Man's way of showing his faithfulness by singing
   C. Celebrations for different seasons
   D. None of the above

7. The intensity of God's wrath increases in sequential order as follows:

   A. Opening of the 7 seals; sounding of the 7 trumpets; pouring out of 7 vials, or bowls
   B. Sounding of the 7 trumpets; opening of the 7 seals; pouring out of 7 vials, or bowls
   C. Pouring out of 7 vials, or bowls; sounding of the 7 trumpets; opening of the 7 seals
   D. Opening of the 7 seals, pouring out of 7 vials, or bowls; sounding of the 7 trumpets

8. The plagues contained in the first six bowls of judgment compare to

   A. The weight of the hailstones and force of the tempests
   B. The earth swallowing up Korah's followers in Numbers 16
   C. The plagues like smallpox, polio, flu, and corona virus
   D. The ten plagues on the Pharoah of Egypt in Exodus chapters 8-10.

9. The greatest earthquake that will ever occur on earth will happen

   A. When the seventh seal is opened
   B. When the seventh trumpet is sounded
   C. When the seventh bowl is poured out
   D. When the Tribulation Period begins

10. Much of Babylon's destruction will be caused by

    A. Grenades, 100lb bombs, and 105 howitzer artillery
    B. A great earthquake and great hail stones
    C. Flooding of the Euphrates River
    D. A nuclear explosion

CHAPTERS 17-19

1. The result of the seventh bowl being poured out caused John to

   A. See the unsaved celebrate since God's wrath is almost finished
   B. See the ones whose names are not in the Book of Life, eat, drink, and be merry
   C. See the ones who rejected Christ to be nonchalantly undisturbed
   D. Marvel with amazement at the spectacle

2. Babylon the Great, the Mother of Harlots and of abominations of the earth

   A. Defines the head of the fallen church in Ephesus
   B. Was seen by John as being drunk with the blood of the saints and martyrs of Jesus
   C. Fell to her knees, cried tears of blood, and asked to be forgiven
   D. Repented and began spreading the Gospel to every nation, tribe, and tongue

3. The seven heads being seven mountains on which the Mother of Harlots sits is located in

   A. New York City although there are no hills there
   B. Babylon in Iraq near the Euphrates River
   C. Rome since there are seven hills there
   D. A place only known for certain by God

4. A one world government is prophesied by the statement in Revelation 17:18:

   A. "That great city which reigns over the kings of the earth"
   B. "The kingdom will be combined to integrate Islam with the church"
   C. "The ruler, Antichrist, is god and king"
   D. None of the above

5. The plagues of death, mourning and famine in Babylon will occur in what length of time?

   A. One month
   B. One week
   C. One day
   D. One hour

6. How long will it take for great riches to come to nothing in the battle of Armageddon?

   A. One month
   B. One week
   C. One day
   D. One hour

7. The connection with the ancient city of Babylon is given by the expression in Revelation 18:5:

   A. "For her sins have reached to heaven"
   B. "The people were becoming more wicked than God had thought they would"
   C. "For the people were speaking many different languages with no interpreters"
   D. "A weather warning predicted man-made climate change"

8. The riders on the white horses in Revelation 6:2 and 19:11 are

   A. Alexander the Great and the Lord Jesus Christ respectively
   B. Satan and the Michael the archangel respectively
   C. The Antichrist and the Lord Jesus Christ, respectively
   D. Elījah and the Moses respectively

9. The word Alleluia in Revelation 19:3 is the Greek equivalent of Hallelujah which means

   A. Eat, drink, and be merry
   B. Peace
   C. Praise Yahweh or Praise the Lord
   D. All of the above

10. The sword out of the Lord's mouth depicts

    A. His omnipotence to be able to hold a sword with His mouth
    B. Great balance and athletic ability
    C. Unbreakable teeth and strong jaw muscles
    D. Judgment through His spoken Word

CHAPTERS 20-22

1. At the end of the battle of Armageddon

   A. Satan will be thrown into the Lake of Fire
   B. The Antichrist will escape and hide in the wilderness
   C. The Antichrist and False Prophet will be cast alive into the Lake of Fire
   D. The False Prophet will escape and hide in the wilderness

2. The Great White Throne is the place for the Lord Jesus to judge:

   A. All believers for rewards
   B. The Antichrist and the false prophet
   C. All those who rejected Him during their lifetime on earth
   D. The false teachers only

3. In Revelation 20:5-6, the first resurrection consists of

   A. Three parts, Christ, the Church, and OT and Tribulation saints' resurrections
   B. The 144,000 being the first to be saved during the Tribulation
   C. Moses and Elījah's resurrections happening first
   D. Enoch's Rapture before all others

4. The Great White Throne Judgment takes place at what time?

   A. Immediately after the battle of Armageddon is won
   B. Immediately after the Antichrist and False Prophet are cast into the Lake of Fire
   C. Before Satan joins the Antichrist and False Prophet in the Lake of Fire
   D. After the thousand years have expired and after Satan is cast into the Lake of Fire

5. The new heaven and new earth will be created at what time?

   A. After Satan is gone and after the Great White Throne Judgment is done
   B. Shortly after the battle of Armageddon
   C. During the thousand years Millennial Reign
   D. When only a few who reject Christ remain

6. The New Jerusalem will be created at what time?

   A. During the thousand years Millennial Reign
   B. When the new heaven and new earth are created
   C. Before the thousand years Millennial Reign
   D. At the end of the Great Tribulation

7. Lord Jesus said on the cross, "It is finished!" and after making all things new, "It is done!"

   A. True
   B. False

8. Unless repenting and sincerely asking to be forgiven, people who have told a lie will have:

   A. A lesser punishment than someone who has committed murder
   B. A lesser punishment than someone who has committed robbery
   C. A lesser punishment than someone who has used God's Name in vain
   D. Their part in the lake which burns with fire and brimstone

9. The reason we have available to us this Book of *The Revelation of Jesus Christ* is:

   A. The angel told John to write these things and not to seal the words of this prophecy
   B. The Bible is a money maker for book sales
   C. We can inform ourselves of all the upcoming catastrophes
   D. We need not be concerned since the warnings are not for us

10. The plagues that are written in this Book will be

    A. Only put upon those who blaspheme God
    B. Added to anyone who adds to or takes away words of this Book
    C. Overcome by man's intellect and ingenuity
    D. None of the above

REVELATION STUDY GUIDE

FINAL EXAM

FINAL EXAM

1. The three passages having to do with the trumpet announcing the Rapture are found in:

   A. 2 Thessalonians 2:1-4, 1 Thessalonians 4:13-18, 1 Corinthians 15:51-52
   B. Revelation 4:1, 1 Thessalonians 4:13-18, Romans 11:25-26
   C. 1 Corinthians 15:51-52, 1 Thessalonians 4:13-18, Revelation 4:1
   D. Revelation 4:1, 1 Thessalonians 4:13-18, 2 Thessalonians 2:7-8

2. What two events must take place prior to the revealing of the Antichrist?

   A. The first half of the Tribulation Period and the Rapture of the Church
   B. Armageddon and the marriage of the Church to the Lamb
   C. The 144,000 Jews sealed and the falling away of faith
   D. The falling away of local churches and the Rapture of the saved Church

3. Where will the marriage supper of the Church to the Lamb take place?

   A. On the present earth since Tribulation believers are resurrected, not raptured
   B. In heaven since all believers including Tribulation believers will be raptured
   C. On the new earth to give the wedding feast a beautiful setting
   D. In Babylon since the participants will be visiting there after Armageddon

4. Why is Babylon called "The Mother of Harlots"? Because:

   A. The city is such a great metropolis
   B. The people there worship idols instead of God
   C. The women there have shaved heads
   D. The people are confused due to all the different languages

5. What are the raptured believers referred to when they praise the Lord for redeeming them?

   A. "Living creatures" in Revelation 5:11
   B. "Disciples" in John 18:2
   C. "Apostates" in 2 Peter 3 and Jude
   D. "Angels" in Revelation 5:8

6. Once sanctified all believers are saved:

   A. For Seven Years only
   B. From wrath only
   C. For eternal life only
   D. From wrath and for eternal life

7. Awards are first given to raptured believers:

   A. Immediately after the Rapture
   B. During the Great Tribulation
   C. During the Millennial Reign
   D. At the Wedding feast

8. The fall and rise of the Babylonian, Medo-Persian, Greek and Roman empires were prophesied by which one of the following:

   A. Isaiah
   B. Jeremiah
   C. Ezekiel
   D. Daniel

9. The trumpet that will announce the Rapture is found in:

   A. Romans 11:25, Revelation 4:1, and 1 Corinthians 15:52
   B. 1 Thessalonians 4:16, 2 Thessalonians 2:7, Revelation 4:1
   C. 1 Corinthians 15:52, 1 Thessalonians 4:16, Revelation 4:1
   D. 1 Corinthians 15:52, 2 Thessalonians 2:7, Revelation 4:1

10. The sounding of a trumpet always signifies the Rapture is imminent.

    A. True
    B. False

11. Those who come to believe during the seven-year Tribulation Period will be:

    A. Persecuted and Raptured
    B. Persecuted, Beheaded and lost forever
    C. Persecuted and survive or be resurrected to life if martyred
    D. None of the above

12. The "living creatures" who recognize the Lord for redeeming them by His blood in Revelation 5:9-11 are

    A. The four living creatures in Revelation 5:8 only
    B. The Cherubim and Seraphim only
    C. The twenty-four elders of the Church only
    D. The ten thousand times ten thousand, and thousands of thousands made up of the many angels, the elders, and Christ's new creation which was recently raptured.

13. The Lord Jesus Christ is acknowledged as the Almighty how many times in Revelation?

    A. At least seven times
    B. Only three times
    C. Twice
    D. Only once

14. The Lord Jesus told John to tell the church of Ephesus how to come back from falling by:

    A. Conducting a revival
    B. Repenting
    C. Worshiping with musical instruments
    D. Preaching how to get more material riches

15. The benefit for reading, hearing and keeping the words of prophecy in the Book of Revelation is:

    A. Blessing
    B. Teaching ability
    C. Discernment
    D. Invitation to the wedding supper

16. Those who accept the mark of the Antichrist beast will be able to repent.

    A. True
    B. False

17. The four horses in Revelation 6 introduce which famous person or persons?

    A. The Lord Jesus
    B. The False Prophet
    C. The Antichrist
    D. All of the above plus Michael the archangel

18. The 144,000 Israelites are saved and sealed

    A. Prior to opening of the first six seals and after revealing of the Antichrist
    B. After the wedding of the Church to the Savior
    C. Prior to the seven-year Tribulation
    D. After the revealing of the Antichrist and after the opening of the sixth seal

19. The intensity of God's wrath increases in sequential order as follows:

    A. Opening of the 7 seals; sounding of the 7 trumpets; pouring out of 7 vials, or bowls
    B. Sounding of the 7 trumpets; opening of the 7 seals; pouring out of 7 vials, or bowls
    C. Pouring out of 7 vials, or bowls; sounding of the 7 trumpets; opening of the 7 seals
    D. Opening of the 7 seals, pouring out of 7 vials, or bowls; sounding of the 7 trumpets

20. The two witnesses in Revelation could quite possibly be:

    A. Two of the 144,000 Israelites who were saved in Revelation 7
    B. The two prophets who appeared in the Transfiguration of Jesus' appearance
    C. Two of the kings of the Northern Kingdom of Israel
    D. Adam and Eve, Job and his wife, or Āhab and Jezebel

21. The "little book" that the angel told John to "eat" represents

    A. Sweet overcoming for those who accept—and the bitter end for those who reject Him
    B. A mystery that is too sacred to be revealed
    C. The bitter beginning and sweet end of the Book of Job
    D. A poetic work of literature

22. The false trinity is made up of which of the following

    A. Caesar, Herod, and Pilate
    B. The Father, Son, and Holy Spirit
    C. Satan, Antichrist, and False Prophet
    D. Serpent, Dragon, and the devil

23. When John visualizes Jesus with a "sharp sickle" in Revelation 14:14, the sickle represents

    A. Harvesting for judgment of the wicked from the just
    B. Harvesting of the believers for the Rapture
    C. A weapon of war to defeat the Antichrist
    D. None of the above

24. The plagues contained in the first six bowls of judgment compare to

    A. The weight of the hailstones and force of the tempests
    B. The earth swallowing up Korah's followers in Numbers 16
    C. The plagues like smallpox, polio, flu, and corona virus
    D. The ten plagues on the Pharoah of Egypt in Exodus chapters 8-10

25. The greatest earthquake that will ever occur on earth will happen

    A. When the seventh seal is opened
    B. When the seventh trumpet is sounded
    C. When the seventh bowl is poured out
    D. When the Tribulation Period begins

26. Babylon's destruction will be caused by

    A. Grenades, 100lb bombs, and 105 howitzer artillery
    B. A great earthquake and great hail stones
    C. Man-made fire
    D. A nuclear explosion

27. Satan, the Antichrist, and the false prophet will simultaneously be thrown into the Lake of Fire.

    A. True
    B. False

28. How long will it take for great riches to come to nothing in the battle of Armageddon?

    A. One month
    B. One week
    C. One day
    D. One hour

29. The riders on the white horses in Revelation 6:2 and 19:11 are

    A. Alexander the Great and the Lord Jesus Christ respectively
    B. Satan and the Michael the archangel respectively
    C. The Antichrist and the Lord Jesus Christ, respectively
    D. Elījah and the Moses respectively

30. The Great White Throne is the place for the Lord Jesus to judge:

    A. All believers for rewards
    B. The Antichrist and the false prophet
    C. All who rejected Him during their lifetime on earth
    D. The false teachers only

REVELATION STUDY GUIDE

CHAPTER EXAM

ANSWERS / REFERENCES

CHAPTER EXAM

ANSWERS / REFERENCES

CHAPTERS 1-3

1.	A	Revelation 1:3
2.	C	Revelation 1:4-5
3.	A	Revelation 1:7; Philippians 2:9-11
4.	D	Revelation 1:12-16; Ezekiel 1:4-28
5.	B	Revelation 2:16
6.	B	Revelation 2:6, 14-15; Numbers 22-25; 31; 1 Timothy 6:5; 2 Peter 2:15; Jude 11b
7.	D	Revelation 2:10
8.	A	Revelation 3:3
9.	B	Revelation 3:8
10.	B	Revelation 4:1-22:16

CHAPTERS 4-7

1.	C	Revelation 1:19-3:22; 4:1
2.	C	Revelation 4:1; 1 Corinthians 15:51-52; 1 Thessalonians 4:13-5:11
3.	D	Revelation 4:4
4.	A	Revelation 5:11
5.	D	Revelation 5:9-11
6.	B	Revelation 6:2-8
7.	A	Revelation 6:2, 4, 8: Daniel. 8:25; 11:21
8.	D	Revelation 6:12; 7:1-8
9.	C	Revelation 7:2-4
10.	A	Revelation 7:9-17

CHAPTERS 8-10

1.	C	Revelation 5:2, 5-7, 9; 8:1
2.	A	Revelation 8:5-13
3.	C	Revelation 8:11
4.	B	Revelation 9:2
5.	B	Revelation 9:5
6.	D	Revelation 9:13-16
7.	A	Revelation 9:20-21
8.	A	Revelation 10:8-10; Ezekiel 3:1-3
9.	C	Revelation 10:6
10.	B	Revelation 10:11

CHAPTERS 11-13

1.	C	Revelation 11:2
2.	B	Revelation 11:6; Exodus. 9:33; 1 Kings 17:1; 18:1; Matthew 17:1-5
3.	D	Revelation 11:12
4.	A	Revelation 11:2; Daniel 9:27
5.	C	Revelation 12:2; Romans 11:25-26
6.	A	Revelation 7:3-4; 12:3-4
7.	D	Revelation 12:7-10
8.	B	Revelation 13:2-10, 11-18
9.	B	Revelation 13:12
10.	A	Revelation 13:15

CHAPTERS 14-16

1.	C	Revelation 7:1-8; 14:1-6
2.	B	Revelation 14:4
3.	A	Revelation 14:1
4.	D	Revelation 14:11
5.	D	Revelation 15:1, 7
6.	A	Revelation 15:3; Exodus 15:1-5, 11, 18; Deuteronomy.26:8
7.	A	Revelation 6:2-16:17
8.	D	Revelation 16:2-13; Exodus 8-10
9.	C	Revelation 16:17-18
10.	B	Revelation. 16:18-21

CHAPTERS 17-19

1.	D	Revelation 17:6
2.	B	Revelation 17:5-6
3.	D	Revelation 17:9
4.	A	Revelation 17:18
5.	C	Revelation 18:8
6.	D	Revelation 18:17
7.	A	Revelation 18:5
8.	C	Revelation 6:2; 19:11
9.	C	Revelation 19:1-6
10.	D	Revelation 19:15; Ephesians 6:17

CHAPTERS 20-22

1.	C	Revelation 16:13-16; 19:20-21; 20:2, 7, 10
2.	C	Revelation 20:11-15
3.	A	Revelation 20:5-6; 1 Corinthians 15:20, 23
4.	D	Revelation 20:7, 10, 11-15
5.	A	Revelation 20:7, 10, 11-15; 21:1
6.	B	Revelation 21:1-2
7.	A	Revelation 21:6; John 19:30
8.	D	Revelation 21:8
9.	A	Revelation 22:10
10.	B	Revelation 22:18-19

REVELATION STUDY GUIDE

FINAL EXAM

ANSWERS / REFERENCES

FINAL EXAM

ANSWERS / REFERENCES

1.	C	1 Corinthians 15:51-52, 1 Thessalonians 4:13-18, Revelation 4:1
2.	D	2 Thessalonians 2:1-3, 6-8
3.	A	Revelation 7:13-14; 14:1-6; 19:9 (Survivors and martyred saints of the Tribulation)
4.	B	Revelation 9:20-21; 17:1-2, 3-6; 18:2-3
5.	A	Revelation 5:9-11
6.	D	Romans 5:9; 1 Thessalonians 1:10; 1 Thessalonians 5:9
7.	A	Revelation 4:4
8.	D	Daniel 8
9.	C	1 Corinthians 15:52, 1 Thessalonians 4:16, Revelation 4:1
10.	B	Revelation 4:1; 8:2-11:15
11.	C	Revelation 7:13-14
12.	D	2 Corinthians 5:17
13.	A	Revelation 1:8; 4:8; 11:17; 15:3; 16:7, 14; 19:15; (21:22)

14.	B	Revelation 2:5
15.	A	Revelation 1:3
16.	B	Revelation 19:20
17.	C	Revelation 6:2-8
18.	D	Revelation 6:12; 7:1-8
19.	A	Revelation 6:2-16:17
20.	B	Revelation 11:6; Exodus 9:33; 1 Kings 17:1; 18:1; Matthew 17:1-5
21.	A	Revelation 10:8-10; Ezekiel 3:1-3
22.	C	Revelation 12-13; 13:4; 2 Thessalonians 2:4, 9; Daniel 11:36-37
23.	A	Revelation 14:14; Matthew 13:37-42
24.	D	Revelation 16:2-13; Exodus Chapters 8-10
25.	C	Revelation 16:17-18
26.	B	Revelation 16:18-21
27.	B	Revelation 19:20; 20:2, 10
28.	D	Revelation 18:17
29.	C	Revelation 6:2; 19:11
30.	C	Revelation 20:11-15

A = 8
B = 7
C = 8
D = 7

Connect with the Author

Check out other Books by the Author:
Website/Blog: https://michaelcopple.com/

Connect with Michael:
Email: mike@michaelcopple.com

www.ingramcontent.com/pod-product-compliance
Lightning Source LLC
Chambersburg PA
CBHW071255070526
44583CB00017B/2473